Time Management 101

Secrets for Succeeding in a Busy World

by

Merrill Douglass

Trade Life Books
Tulsa, Oklahoma

All unattributed quotations were written by the author.

Time Management 101:
Secrets for Succeeding in a Busy World
ISBN 1-57757-037-5
Copyright © 1998 by Merrill Douglass

Published by Trade Life Books
P.O. Box 55388
Tulsa, OK 74155

Introduction

My friend Charles "Tremendous" Jones says, "You are the same as you'll be in five years except for two things: the people you meet and the books you read." This book is dedicated to him.

Nearly everyone likes short, pithy quotes that tackle the issues of our lives. We clip them out, e-mail them to friends, stick them on our refrigerators, or write them on the pages of our daily calendars.

Over the years, I have specialized in helping people accomplish more with their time. In the process of my work I have gathered hundreds of powerful quotations that have helped inspire my clients—and me—to better manage our lives. I know the quotes, along with my to-the-point commentary, will challenge you to master the way you use this wonderful gift called "time."

Merrill Douglass

I wish I could stand on
a busy corner and beg
people to give me all
their wasted hours.

Bernard Berenson

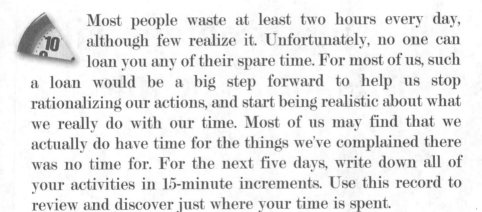

Most people waste at least two hours every day, although few realize it. Unfortunately, no one can loan you any of their spare time. For most of us, such a loan would be a big step forward to help us stop rationalizing our actions, and start being realistic about what we really do with our time. Most of us may find that we actually do have time for the things we've complained there was no time for. For the next five days, write down all of your activities in 15-minute increments. Use this record to review and discover just where your time is spent.

The only problem with this job is people.

Anonymous

If you work in an office, you probably have people dropping in on you all day long. Some are worthwhile visits, but many are probably a waste of time. In anticipating your daily schedule, be sure to allow enough time for those interruptions and other unscheduled events. Most of us need to allow at least 25 percent of the day for these interruptions. If you allow for them in your day, you will be less frustrated when they do occur. Also, allow for some quiet time when you make yourself unavailable for an hour or so. Use this quiet time to work on the important jobs that require concentration.

Ask yourself often:
Will what I am doing
right now help me
achieve my goals?

Whatever you do will either help or hurt your efforts to accomplish your goals. Once your time is spent, it can't be recovered. Many of us just assume that whatever it is we're doing needs to be done. The key to top performance is to make the most of whatever time you have. If the answer to the question of whether you are achieving your goals with an activity is "no," then switch to something that will contribute to them. Ask this question often, and you'll achieve greater accomplishments than at any other time in your life through a renewed sense of purpose.

A positive attitude will almost always make things work out better.

You probably know that approaching just about anything with a positive attitude helps, but you may still have an underlying negative attitude toward time. For instance, do you think that time works against you, that there aren't enough hours in a day, that time is running out and you won't make it? Instead, say to yourself that you have enough time, that time can be on your side, that you will make it. Good time management begins with a positive attitude—believing that you can manage it well.

If I had eight hours to cut down a tree, I'd spend six sharpening my axe.

Abraham Lincoln

Smart woodcutters don't keep chopping away at the trees all day long; they take time to sharpen their axe. With a sharp tool you can get more work done in less time with less effort. Do you take time to sharpen your time management axe, or are you chopping with a dull blade? Sharpening your time management axe means perfecting the skills and techniques that good time management demands. Plan to set aside time every week to improve your time management capacity in some way.

Clutter expands to fill the space available for its retention.

Douglass' Law of Clutter

You don't have to choose between neatness and disaster—the key is balance. Neatness, overdone, becomes a ridiculous obsession. A little clutter never hurt anyone. But clutter, overdone, becomes a terrific time waster. It hinders your performance and causes other people to think less of you. For starters, don't allow your desktop or work area to become a catchall. Return or file work where it belongs. The consistent use of this old advice can help you create new work habits.

More people get bitten by mosquitoes than elephants.

Joel Weldon

Most of us don't forget the big issues of our work, it's the little things that tend to slip through the cracks. Yet, overlooking these little things can be as disastrous as forgetting the bigger issues. Little things left undone, or not done at the right time, can jeopardize an entire project. Simple as it sounds, many people would be further ahead if they would make lists and write memos more often. A note is usually better than memory.

Most people are more concerned with doing things right than with doing the right things.

Peter Drucker

Peter Drucker is considering the difference between efficiency and effectiveness. He says that often we focus on the wrong details first. We assume that the key to greater productivity is to do whatever we're doing more efficiently; that is, do it faster or cheaper. Drucker says that's actually backwards. First, we need to ask, "What are the right things to do, what actions are necessary to reach the goal?" Then, ask "What are the right ways to do them?" The secret is to focus on doing the right things right.

Ninety-five percent of all the things put in filing cabinets are never looked at again by anyone.

Why do we keep so much stuff? Most people tell me they save things because "you never know when they'll come in handy." That's right only 5 percent of the time. A better approach is to develop a definite criteria for making decisions on what to keep and what to throw out. Do you really need it? What is the worst thing that could happen if you didn't keep it? How are you likely to use it again? Is there a legal requirement for keeping it? I say the bottom line ought to be, if you haven't used something in six months or so—get rid of it!

Successful people form the habit of doing what failures don't like to do.

Earl Nightingale

Call it willpower, discipline, determination, or anything else you like, successful people are different. They will do things they don't necessarily like to do in order to get the results they want. Failures, though, will accept whatever results are possible by doing only what they like to do. Successful people are motivated by pleasing results, while failures are motivated by pleasing methods. All of us have to choose real success for ourselves.

SIX THINGS THAT TIME IS

Perishable
Expensive
Measurable
Continuous
Irreversible
Irreplaceable

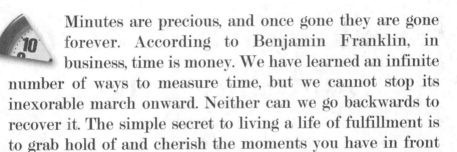

Minutes are precious, and once gone they are gone forever. According to Benjamin Franklin, in business, time is money. We have learned an infinite number of ways to measure time, but we cannot stop its inexorable march onward. Neither can we go backwards to recover it. The simple secret to living a life of fulfillment is to grab hold of and cherish the moments you have in front of you, beginning this very second.

We have met the enemy, and they is us.

Pogo

Too often our personal order for the day is a quick fix consisting of some gimmick that requires no change or commitment on our part. We want something easy to use and guaranteed to work. Something that will solve all of our problems—a panacea—but there is none. We find ourselves blaming others for our shortcomings, when the real culprit is ourselves. All improvement requires hard work, yet most of us aren't very fond of that kind of work. We prefer taking the easy way out. It's our habits that lie at the heart of the issue.

Organizing is what you do before you do something else so that when you do it, it won't be all messed up.

Winnie the Pooh

Getting organized is like having a game plan. Any coach can tell you that your chances of winning are better if you have such a plan. Organizing the details of your life is what creates your game plan. Organizing makes you productive. To get better organized ask, "What do we want to accomplish?" "What needs to be done?" "When should it be done?" "How should it be done?" "Who should do it?" "How long will it take to do it?" "When should it be started?"

Knowing is not enough; we must apply. Willing is not enough; we must do.

Goethe

Results usually depend more on what you do than on what you know. It is not enough to know; you must also act. Knowledge without action is impotent. Good results require more than just good intentions. Someone said that the road to hell is paved with good intentions. What you need is the habit of digging in and doing. Instead of saying, "Why doesn't someone do something about that?" just go ahead and do something about it yourself.

The more you do of what you're doing, the more you'll get of what you're getting.

Grandmother's Proverb

Many people fantasize about a time when everything will work out great for them—like winning a sweepstakes. But it's more often our habits that determine our futures, not fate. Too many people say they'd change, if only something else would happen first. But that's backward. If you want something different in your life, you'll have to change in some way now. Once you change, then new opportunities open up for you. But if you don't change, then your future will look very much the same as your past.

There is always a better way to do anything.

Thomas Edison

In 1963, I met Bill Mogensen, who sold me on the simple idea he called "Work Simplification." The main idea, he said, was to find at least one way to improve our jobs every week. That's fifty-two improvements every year. To see this happen requires constantly analyzing what we are doing and looking for ways to improve. The payoff, however, is when we discover that we have formed a habit of self-improvement. At that point, it's easy to keep things moving upward.

We spend most of our waking hours with information.

Linda Lederman
Communications in the Workplace

In one year, the average American will read or complete 3000 notices and forms, scan 100 newspapers and 36 magazines, watch 2463 hours of television, listen to 730 hours of radio, buy 20 recordings, talk on the telephone almost 61 hours, read 3 books, and spend countless hours exchanging information in conversation. No wonder we have information overload. Since time is so precious, think carefully about which information you really need and that which is unproductive. Then simply expose yourself to the information that has value and ignore the rest.

95 out of 100 people never take advantage of shortcuts learned by others' experience.

Quincy Munford
Librarian of Congress

So many of us continue to do things the hard way. Often, this is because we don't know that the information we need is available, or where to get it quickly and effectively. Many of us have not learned how to take advantage of the advances in technology that place an increasing amount of information and know-how at our fingertips. Because we don't take advantage of the shortcuts that are available, we wind up wasting a lot of time and effort. Make it a habit to spend time each week discovering new sources of information that will maximize your effectiveness.

Keep interruptions short and you will solve a huge part of your time problem.

You can't stop interruptions from happening, but too many routine disturbances will ruin your plans for the day. While you can't prevent all interruptions from happening, you can help determine how long they last. Try all kinds of strategies. Stand up, put a big clock in your work space, tell people you're busy, ask people to bunch things together, and close your door. Consider asking the people who interrupt you the most for their input on how to minimize disturbances.

Dost thou love life?
Then do not waste time,
for that's the stuff life
is made of.

Benjamin Franklin

The way you spend your time defines the life you live. To waste your time is to waste your life. To change your life, change the way you spend your time. Time is more than just a work issue; it's also a life issue. The key is to live a balanced life, spending an adequate amount of time in all aspects of your life: spiritual, family, community, social, career, self-development, health, leisure. Keep a time log to find out how your life-time is allocated. What parts of your life get too much time? Where do you need more time? You only have one life. Make it count.

You can't no more do what
you ain't prepared for, than
you can come back from
where you ain't been.

Robert Henry

Tackling situations without any forethought is like diving into a swimming pool without first checking for water. Good results depend less on luck and more on planning. Actually, chance favors the person who is prepared. Forget about luck and learn how to plan better. For starters, write out a weekly plan. Answer these five questions: (1) What results do you intend to achieve this week? (2) What must you do to get these results? (3) What are the priorities? (4) How much time will each activity require? (5) When will you do each activity?

SIX CLICHÉS ABOUT TIME

Time flies.
Time is money.
Time marches on.
Time and time again.
Time heals all wounds.
Time waits for no man.

Clichés are truths repeated so often that no one pays much attention to them anymore. They may be overly familiar and trite, but they still contain truth. Look at these six statements with new insight. For example: How much money is your time worth? What wounds have been healed with time? Draw your own questions from these clichés to discover how they apply to your life.

Winners focus, losers spray.

Sidney Harris

Winners focus on the results they want to achieve. In so doing, they are able to see what does or doesn't contribute to their goals, and avoid the things that don't help. Losers, on the other hand, focus on all the tasks in front of them. Without a clear-cut way of sorting through all the trivia, they wind up being pushed and pulled by whatever happens. The key to staying focused is having a clear vision of what you're after, and ignoring everything else.

Happiness is an unlisted telephone number.

Telephones are both a plus and a minus in our lives. We can't work without them, but there are times when we wish they weren't such a bother. Here are some tips to help you better control your calls: (1) Get through the small talk as quickly as possible. Get right to the point and stay there. (2) Bring calls to a prompt close. Be firm, but don't be rude. (3) Tell people who call you regularly when you prefer to receive calls, or when you are most likely to be in. (4) Record and analyze your telephone calls periodically to find out what is really happening. (5) Plan your calls. Organize your thoughts and questions beforehand; have all pertinent information at hand, and know what you are going to say. Unplanned calls waste 35 percent more of your time.

Work expands to fill the time available.

Parkinson's Law

Time and human behavior mix together in some amazing ways. For example, whether you allow a lot or a little time for a job, it will probably take whatever time you've allowed. If you allow more time than you actually need, you'll use everything you've allowed anyway. The key to getting more done in less time is to carefully consider just how long it actually takes to do the job, and then not budget a single second more than that.

Time is basic; unless it is managed, nothing else can be managed.

Peter Drucker

Peter Drucker points out that time is all you have to work with. Saying you didn't have enough time is probably admitting that you didn't manage the time you had. However, when you're out of time, all your other skills are of no value. You simply have to control time to get good results. The familiar term "time management" is actually a misnomer, because no one can manage time. What you really manage is yourself. Managing time simply means managing yourself in order to accomplish your goals within the time available.

Just because it's urgent doesn't mean it's important.

Most of us have learned to respond to urgent activities, but not necessarily to important activities. To break the tyranny of the urgent, learn to distinguish what is: (a) important and urgent; (b) important, but not urgent; (c) urgent, but not important; (d) neither important nor urgent. The highest payoffs and greatest opportunities are usually important, but not urgent. Focus first on what's important, not what's merely urgent.

There are two rules for achieving anything. Rule No. 1: Get started. Rule No. 2: Keep going.

Howard Hunt

Lots of people say they intend to get something done, but for one reason or another they never get around to it. Some say they are waiting for the right moment, but that moment never seems to arrive. And there are some people who quit when the going gets a little tough. When the chips are down, it isn't talent, brilliance, or education, but persistence that pays off. Develop the habit of persistence and there will be very little that you can't accomplish.

Time is man's most precious asset. All men neglect it; all regret the loss of it; nothing can be done without it.

Voltaire

In today's vernacular, too many of us "talk the talk," but we don't "walk the walk." We cry and complain and moan about how much time we don't have. And it's true, when our time's up, we're done, whether we want to be or not. If time really is our critical resource, why don't we act like it? We'd be better off to stop complaining and start focusing on how to make the most of the time we have.

Nothing ever happens in
your life unless you
create the space for it
to happen in.

James McCay

Life is a zero-sum game. Here you are, spending all the time you have on something that's really important, but it's impossible to add a new activity into your life until you first subtract an old activity. That's what McCay means by "creating space." To find the time for the new thing, you have to reduce or eliminate the old thing. If you pick a specific time for doing the new thing, you increase the probability that you will actually do it.

Besides the noble art of getting things done, there is the noble art of leaving things undone. The wisdom of life lies in eliminating the nonessentials.

Chinese Proverb

There are two kinds of activities—essential and non-essential. Essential activities are those that must be done to achieve a particular result. Nonessential activities are just that—they do not have to be done, and neither do they contribute to the desired result. Discover what you're doing that is nonessential and replace it with essentials. Your effectiveness will soar. Most people make a to-do list (essentials), but you might also try making a not-to-do list (nonessentials).

There are only four things you can do with paper: dump it, delegate it, do it, or delay it.

Do your best to resist paper. Most of us are actually drawn to paper, as if it were some kind of security blanket. Experts estimate we could throw out 40-50 percent of our paper and never miss it. When in doubt—throw it out. Or, at least use a "Maybe" box. Work on important paper, throw away junk paper, put everything else in the "Maybe" box. If anyone ever asks for it, you'll know where it is. When the box gets full, dump it. When you do act on paper, try to handle each piece of paper only once. Do whatever needs to be done the first time you pick it up. Don't set it aside without taking some action on it.

All work and no play makes Jack a dull boy.

Old English Proverb

We all need some time off to recharge our batteries. There are times when we ought to ease back and relax. No one should work all the time. Take lots of "vacations." An increasing number of people spend too much time with their jobs, and not enough time away from the job. And, when you do get away, don't take any part of the job with you.

THREE APHORISMS ABOUT TIME

1. You will never find time for anything.
2. If you want time, you must make it.
3. You cannot add until you first subtract.

Stop trying to "find" time, and concentrate on how to "make" time. Making time is largely a matter of reducing or eliminating activities. If you're unwilling to give up anything, you will never have time for something else. Do your adding and subtracting on the basis of importance. Ask yourself: What will contribute the most to what I'm trying to accomplish?

When you choose a habit you also choose the results of that habit.

Zig Ziglar

Most of our behavior is controlled by habit patterns. A habit can be good if it helps you achieve your goals; it is bad if it hinders your goals. It is much easier to achieve good results when your habits work with you rather than against you. So, keep the good habits and replace the bad ones. A success secret: most work-related habits can be changed within three to four weeks. To create new habits, begin as strongly as you can, tell others what you are doing, and ask them to help you change.

Plant a thought, harvest an act;
plant an act, harvest a habit;
plant a habit, harvest a character;
plant a character,
harvest a destiny.

Native American Proverb

Nothing just happens. Embedded within life is the law of cause and effect. Today's dynamics are the result of a process that takes place over time. There is actually a method to what sometimes appears as madness. Outcomes, or results, start with thoughts, which produce actions, which become habits, which define who we are, which help determine what happens to us. Every day, in lots of little ways, we build the pathway we will travel to the end of our journey.

Socializing is like aspirin—a little helps a lot, but too much can be deadly.

Excessive socializing is a major problem in most organizations. Walk the halls at almost any time and chances are you'll find people standing or sitting around chatting with each other. Excessive socializing is a big reason why many people have to work late or take their work home with them. Don't fall into the trap of rationalizing that all socializing is beneficial.

Whether you think you can, or whether you think you can't, you're right.

Henry Ford

Psychologists have identified a group of people they call internals—people who believe they can control events in their lives; that they really can win regardless of what others might say. The more you think you can control, the more likely you are to try, and inevitably, the more you will have a positive impact on real life. The message is clear—yes you can, if you think you can! Make a habit of focusing on the "Yes, I can!" attitude.

Men of lofty genius, when they are doing the least work, are the most active.

Leonardo da Vinci

Busy has become a virtue, yet being busy doesn't necessarily mean achieving results. This notion is instilled early in life and continually reinforced by those who try to keep us "busy." Few of us are encouraged to spend more time thinking. "Just keep busy." Even physical activity is more valued than mental activity. I won't argue against a good regimen of exercise, but it is positive mental activity that produces the greatest results. You will find that the more—and more positively—you think, the more time you have.

Procrastination and indecision are twins.

Anonymous

Indecision is a major cause of procrastination. There is a time to deliberate and a time to act. The time for action is when further information will add little to the quality of the decision. Make a sincere effort to obtain the best information possible within the time available. Weigh the pros and cons. Then make the decision and move on.

Man must sit on a chair for a long time before roast duck flies in.

Chinese Proverb

Some folks explain someone else's success as "good luck," as if it was simply a fortunate fate that cast favor on them. That's plain baloney. Ann Landers once said that good luck was that point in the road where preparation and opportunity came together. Most folks, she said, failed to recognize it because it came disguised as hard work. The message is clear: If you want roast duck, you'll have to catch the duck and cook it.

Somehow, I can't help
questioning the ability,
the efficiency, the dependability
of any person who is
habitually late.

B. C. Forbes

Mr. Forbes' opinion is wider spread than most workers suspect. Those who are continuously tardy are not respected—pure and simple! Developing the habit of being on time is one of the best things you'll ever do for your career. It simply means that no one will ever wait for you if it's within your power to control it. Show up at meetings on time; deliver your part of the work on time; be ready to receive your appointments on time; develop a reputation for always being on time with everything. One way to do this: focus on the time you must leave, not when you want to arrive.

Anyone can do any amount of work, provided it isn't the work he is supposed to be doing at that moment.

Robert Benchley

I've dusted my desk and I've wound up my watch,
I've tightened (then loosened) my belt by a notch,
I've polished my glasses, removed a small speck,
I've looked at my check stubs to check out a check,
I've searched for my tweezers and pulled out a hair,
I've opened a window to let in some air,
I've straightened a picture, I've swatted a fly,
I've looked for a book and I've straightened my tie,
I've sharpened each pencil till sharp as a dirk . . .
I've run out of reasons for not starting work.

Anonymous

Having respect for your own time will assure respect for the other person's time.

Robert Half

A complaint that we all hear rather often today is, "Nobody respects my time!" Perhaps a major reason for this complaint is that so few of us seem to respect our own time. If we did, maybe the people around us would change, too. We teach best by example. So, first show respect for your own time, and then show respect for other people's time. Before long, others will treat you differently.

SIX COMMON TIME PROBLEMS

Telephones
Meetings
Paperwork
Visitors
Procrastination
"Firefighting"

Everyone of us wastes time. Even the most self-disciplined have wasted moments now and then. But there is a difference between the people who consistently produce good results and those who don't. The producers manage to hold their wasted time to a minimum. They have learned to control the controllable and allow for the uncontrollable. A good rule to follow is to eliminate one personal time waster every week. In a few weeks, eliminating these wasters will become a good habit.

You can do an adequate job in about 10 percent of the time it takes to do a perfect job.

Perfectionists spend enormous amounts of time arranging and rearranging, yet rarely achieve perfection. They often get sidetracked on the minor points that are almost insignificant. To reduce a perfectionistic tendency, practice striving for "good" performance instead of "best" performance. This is not suggesting "sloppy" work, but is suggesting that you spend an appropriate amount of time for what the job is worth. Remember that most of us are paid to get results, not to be perfect.

The hurrieder I go, the behinder I get.

Pennsylvania Dutch Observation

Everything about life and work seems to be whirling faster and faster, until the bywords of our day are, "hurry, hurry, hurry . . . go, go, go." Great swarms of people are always in a rush, always on the go, always doing something, never relaxed; rushaholics suffering from hurryitis. They wear you out just watching them. Rushing around so much would indicate they have no firm direction, and over the long run they usually accomplish less than all their busyness would indicate. It's better to slow down a bit, build breaks into your routine, take time to think, and practice patience. Constant activity does not automatically mean greater effectiveness and efficiency.

When you have a number of disagreeable duties to perform, always do the most disagreeable first.

Josiah Quincy

This is mother's "eat your spinach first" approach. It works well, even though most of us don't want to do it this way. Most of us seem to approach life with the attitude, "Do the fun part first, because the rest of the day is probably going to be a drudge." How much better it would be to do the disagreeable first, and discover that the rest of the day can be a pleasure. What's more, the disagreeable is often more important, so you also make more significant progress.

The more important an item, the less likely it is urgent, and the more urgent an item, the less likely it is important.

Dwight D. Eisenhower

Everyone seems to be living in a tension between the important and the urgent. Importance is relative to goals; urgency is relative to time. Important issues are those that help you achieve your goals. Important issues tend to have long-term consequences, while urgent things tend to have short-term consequences. Urgent things may or may not relate to goals, but they are always more demanding. Therefore, urgent issues tend to crowd out important things. Learn to focus on important, and ignore urgent.

Plan your work, and work your plan.

Norman Vincent Peale

No road map will guarantee your arrival at a destination. It's not enough to point your car in the right direction; it is necessary to turn the ignition key and step on the accelerator. Some of us seem to think that making a plan is all that's needed to arrive at a goal— that somehow everything will automatically work out. Making a plan is certainly a noble beginning, but every mile will bring a flood of potential detours. Every mile along the highway of life demands a sense of determination to make the plan work—determination and a certain amount of shifting and regrouping—but never surrender.

Time is like money; the less we have of it to spare the further we make it go.

Josh Billings

One of the most deadly beliefs for the person attempting to successfully manage time is the mistaken notion there is always plenty of time for any deadline. The further off the deadline, the more mistaken the notion. However, the truth is, we all have less time than we think we have. For instance, unexpected issues we can't control take 25-50 percent of every day. One of the big values of careful planning and reckoning is that it makes us aware of how much time we do not have. Once we realize how little time we actually have, we are far more likely to take greater care in how we spend it.

The man with two clocks never knows for sure what time it is.

Chinese Proverb

This same truth also applies to calendars and lists. Use only one calendar. If you have two calendars you never know for sure what your commitments and schedules really are. Put personal and work things on the same calendar. And, make just one to-do list, with both work and personal items on the list. Otherwise, if you try to use multiple calendars and lists, the personal side of your life will inevitably get crowded out by work. There's only one you, and you only have one life; you only need one calendar and one list.

This time, like all times,
is a very good one,
if we but know what
to do with it.

Ralph Waldo Emerson

Because we always have so much to do, or so it seems, we don't often consider what we actually should do. To make matters worse, many of us waste our precious moments focusing on the past or the future. We must learn to live in the present, which is all we really ever have. Make good use of the present, day after day, and you will undoubtedly have a great future.

It has been my
observation that most
people get ahead during
the time that others waste.

Henry Ford

Each of us is given the same amount of time every day. Yet, some people seem to be able to accomplish much more with their hours than others. The difference? Those who accomplish more manage to waste less of their time than others do. It has been said that the difference between success and failure is about two hours a day. The willingness to do that extra "something" makes all the difference in the world.

SIX WAYS YOU KNOW THAT A MEETING WAS A WASTE OF TIME

There was no agenda.

It started late.

No decisions were reached.

You forgot what it was about.

You anticipated the coffee break.

You are considering framing your doodles.

Making a meeting productive remains one of the biggest challenges in most organizations. Here are a few hints for meeting success: Don't meet without a good reason. Make an agenda and stick to it. Start on time, stay on time, and end on time. Don't invite too many people. Make sure the right people are there. Apply a little common sense and you can easily change your meeting habits.

He who every morning plans the transaction of the day and follows out the plan, carries a thread that will guide him through the labyrinth of the most busy life.

Victor Hugo

To manage time well requires that we create and maintain a good set of habits. Daily planning is one of the best. Another is weekly planning. By pushing the horizon out for several days, it is actually easier to smooth our today. Seeing how the days are related to each other makes it easier to choose the right activities today. Our plans then become the "curbs" that keep us on the right road.

We realize that our dilemma
goes deeper than a shortage
of time; it is basically a problem
of priorities.

Charles E. Hummel

Nearly every day at sunset many of us realize that we have left undone those things that we ought to have done; and we have done those things which we ought to have left undone. Truth is, most of us are driven by the urgent events in our lives, what Charles Hummel calls the "tyranny of the urgent." The only way to break out of that trap is to force ourselves to ignore the urgent and focus on what's really important—our most critical priorities.

Life is too important to be taken seriously.

Chinese Proverb

If you ask me, some folks are simply too uptight these days—everything is a major issue. They never seem to relax; they never cut themselves any slack. What's my advice for them? Learn to go with the flow of life. Having your own way all the time is really not very important in the grand scheme of things. Pride and greed are tremendous time wasters, which also destroy relationships and organizations. Learn to avoid them. Learn to laugh at yourself and your situation. Above all, maintain a proper perspective. Remember, no matter what you do, you'll never get out of life alive.

The reason most major goals are not achieved is that we spend our time doing second things first.

Anonymous

Here are several common ways to do second things first: (1) doing what you enjoy before doing what you don't enjoy; (2) doing the easy job before the hard job; (3) doing quick tasks before time-consuming tasks; (4) responding to the demands of others before your own demands; (5) waiting until the deadline approaches to get started; (6) doing interesting jobs before uninteresting jobs; (7) doing things that provide immediate closure; (8) doing small jobs before large jobs.

Do any of these sound familiar? If you can claim any of these bad priority habits, you ought to consider changing your ways. Train yourself to start with first things first, and you'll automatically achieve more.

Reduce your plan to writing.
The moment you complete this,
you will have definitely given
concrete form to the
intangible desire.

Napoleon Hill

There are people who actually believe that they have minds like steel traps; they don't have to make themselves lists or write themselves memos or reminders; they seem to think they can keep their plans in their head. Still, with all the hectic, fragmented, pressured days many of us face, those thoughts are quickly pushed to the back of your mind. They often surface only at the end of the day when you have time to pause and reflect. By then, it's too late to do anything about them. Don't take unnecessary chances. Writing your plan down is a big step to making sure it happens.

When you don't know where you're going, any road will take you there.

Cheshire Cat
Alice in Wonderland

In order to figure out what's really important, you must first have a goal, some desired outcome or intended result. Activity is important only when it helps you move toward your goal. If you haven't defined the goal, then how can you determine what is important? Without a goal, it doesn't matter what you do.

Either we work or meet; we can't do both.

Peter Drucker

It's positively too easy to call a meeting. And to make matters worse, many of those meetings are simply not productive. They should never have happened in the first place. So, my advice is, before you call another meeting, pause and consider whether it's really necessary. Consider the consequences of not having the meeting. Make decisions without meetings, and never use a committee or group if it can be done by an individual. Consider alternatives to meetings, such as memos, conference calls, voice mail, electronic mail or fax machines. If you do decide to have a meeting, make an agenda and stick to it. At the end of the meeting, make sure everyone knows what must be done, who will do it, and when it is due.

An unfortunate thing about this world is that the good habits are much easier to give up than the bad ones.

W. Somerset Maugham

Mr. Maugham's remark is to be taken as satire, but it's true! It's one of the mysteries of life. I don't know why it's true, why it happens, but it is and it does. I feel it as much as anyone. The cure? A bit of self-discipline will enable us to do what we know we should do, whether or not we feel like doing it. The good news is that we don't have to give up good habits—including the habit of self-discipline.

Every man living can do more than he thinks he can.

Henry Ford

Several studies show that the average worker is productive for only 54 percent of the day—a definite indication that most of us can just about double our output. A major key to productivity is to analyze and plan carefully. Another key is to raise your expectations with what I call the "Rule of One More." It means adding one more worthwhile activity to your daily list. For example, almost every sales person could make one more call every day than what he or she is currently doing. Try it for yourself and see the positive results.

Before going to bed every night, tear a page from the calendar, and say, "There goes another day of my life, never to return."

This is a graphic exercise to help you become more conscious of time. Exaggerate your actions by tearing the page off with a vengeance, crumple it into a ball, then throw it forcefully into the wastebasket. The key to this exercise is to ask yourself: What did I accomplish today that was worthwhile? Or maybe even better is the question: What did you get for your "payment" of a day?

SIX THINGS YOU CAN DO TO IMPROVE TIME MANAGEMENT

Analyze time spent.
Clarify priorities.
Create a planning system.
Perform the important first.
Jump to it with an early start.
Do it now!

To analyze time spent, keep a time record for a week or two. To clarify your priorities, identify the degree of importance and urgency for each task. To improve your planning, develop the habit of writing out a weekly plan for what you want to accomplish. Always start with the most important tasks first. To get an early start, get up earlier, or maybe it's more realistic to suggest that you start working when you get to work. Learn to change your do-it-later urge into a do-it-now habit.

Nothing is particularly hard if you divide it into small jobs.

Henry Ford

When looking at the big picture, there are those who respond with a paralysis of inaction. To these folks the experience is so overwhelming that they don't know where to start. That's when a detailed step-by-step plan of action needs to be developed. You see, when big pictures are broken down into smaller components, they become more believable. Focus on the first step in achieving the big picture—that step should be small enough not to overwhelm. The next step will be obvious, as will the following one. Proceeding step by step, you can accomplish even the most overwhelming projects. Big achievements are made up of lots of little steps. In other words, "Yard by yard, life is hard; but inch by inch, life's a cinch."

SIX TOOLS FOR EFFECTIVE TIME MANAGEMENT

A computer
A calendar
A "tickler file"
A wastepaper basket
A "maybe" box
A door

A computer does many chores faster. A calendar keeps track of appointments and deadlines. A "tickler file" is a reminder file—a way of storing things until they are needed without losing track of them. A wastebasket is a place for junk. A "maybe box" is for papers you're not sure about. A door allows you quiet time to concentrate on important work.

The value of time is in everybody's mouth, but in few people's practice.

Lord Chesterfield

Everywhere I go people talk to me about their time problems, yet few of them are actually trying to improve their situation. Lots of complaints, little action. Frankly, I think time has become a bit like the weather—we talk a lot about it, but we don't believe anything can be done about it. At least we don't try. Actually, I think most people know more about good time management than they're using. They know what to do, but they aren't doing it. I wonder why? Talk is cheap. Action yields priceless rewards.

Priorities: think of what you're doin',
Priorities: you may soon be bluin',
Priorities: you'll drive yourself
to ruin,
If you pick the wrong priorities.

Avery Schreiber

Some people claim that always working on the basis of priorities isn't possible. Yet, it is not only possible, it is essential. There is no other way to gain control of your time. Not everything is equally important, but if you fail to establish and follow priorities, you guarantee that you will spend an increasing amount of time on work of lower value and have much less to show for your efforts.

Time is a paradox: you never seem to have enough of it, yet in reality, you have all the time there is.

Most of us face a daily dilemma: too much work and not enough time. Truth is, there is always more to do than time will allow. That's why we have to make choices. The problem is not a shortage of time, but how you choose to use the time available. You can't get any more time, but you can learn to make better choices. Remember, too, that there is always enough time for the really important things.

80 percent of the value comes from 20 percent of the items.

The 80/20 Rule

So much of what we do can be called trivial. Only a few things are really critical. Can you differentiate between the two? Even a small increase in critical activities will produce a huge result, while lots of time spent on trivial things will probably produce very little result. Learn to recognize what the few critical things are in your own job. Concentrate on them and try to spend more of your time on them.

SIX THINGS YOU CANNOT DO WITH TIME

Save it.
Buy it.
Borrow it.
Steal it.
Manufacture it.
Modify it.

Many people refer to time as a resource, something that lies ready for use, something that can be called on for aid. Time is like that, but it's also a very different kind of resource. The only thing you can do with time is spend it. Unlike other resources, if you don't use it, it disappears anyway. Stop thinking about how to "save" time and start thinking about how to "spend" it wisely.

You must make time for your opportunities as well as your problems.

Peter Drucker

Most of us don't have much trouble finding time to care for crises and problems. Many of us are prone to dropping everything in order to care for the crisis. I wonder how many people have difficulty finding time to pursue new opportunities, but never think of applying the same habit they use for crises. What do you say? Why not simply drop everything and make time for the opportunity? If it's important enough, that makes good sense.

It is better to ask some of the questions than to know all the answers.

James Thurber

This book is as much about questions as it is answers. Here are several excellent questions to ask yourself at this point in your reading: How do I waste my own time? How do I waste your time? How can I become more effective? How could I help you be more effective? How could we improve our procedures? What's the single greatest time management tool I've picked up from reading this book? The better your questions, the better your answers.

If I ignore it, will I get fired?

T. Frank Hardesty

Most people start the day tackling the quick, easy, or enjoyable tasks first. This quickly becomes a habit. Yet, a simple question can bring amazing clarity. Asking Frank's question will help you eliminate lots of useless paper, avoid many trivial tasks, and get you focused on what adds value and what doesn't.

Bunch routine items together for handling at one time so you won't interrupt others as much.

Although interruptions are the top time waster in most offices, the majority of them involve routine or trivial issues. They could easily be bunched together. The payoff? Bunched items only take about 25 percent as much time as handling them one at a time. If we all bunched routine items, everyone would have fewer interruptions.

About the Author

Dr. Merrill Douglass is Dean of the School of Professional Programs at Shorter College in Marietta, Georgia. He is an internationally recognized expert in time management, having conducted over 3000 time management seminars for corporate clients.

Dr. Douglass is the author of several books, including *Success Secrets* (published by Honor Books), *Manage Your Time Your Work Yourself*, and *Time Management for Teams*. His books have been translated into five languages. His cassette tape album, *The New Time Management*, was a best-seller. Dr. Douglass has also written hundreds of articles for magazines and journals, newspaper columns, and daily radio commentaries.

In his consulting and seminar work, Dr. Douglass draws upon a varied background in business and education. He has many years of practical experience as a successful manager and entrepreneur, and has also been a professor at several universities. He earned his doctorate from Indiana University, with a double major in Management and Organizational Behavior.

For more information about seminars, consulting services, or to write the author, please send your correspondence to:

Dr. Merrill Douglass
1401 Johnson Ferry Road, Suite 328
Marietta, GA 30062
770-973-3977 (Tel) • 770-973-4603 (Fax)

This and other titles by Merrill Douglass
are available from your local bookstore.

Other titles available in the 101 Series:

Manhood 101, Edwin Louis Cole
New Leadership 101, John Maxwell
Relationships 101, Les & Leslie Parrott
Winning 101, Van Crouch